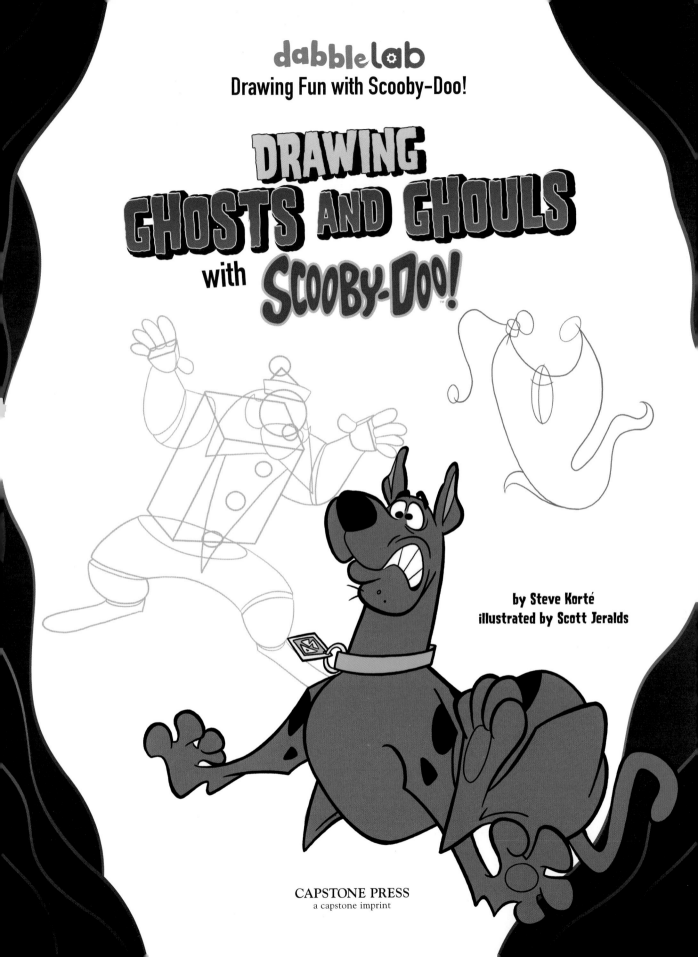

dabblelab
Drawing Fun with Scooby-Doo!

DRAWING GHOSTS AND GHOULS
with SCOOBY-DOO!

by Steve Korté
illustrated by Scott Jeralds

CAPSTONE PRESS
a capstone imprint

Published by Capstone Press, an imprint of Capstone.
1710 Roe Crest Drive
North Mankato, Minnesota 56003
capstonepub.com

Library of Congress Cataloging-in-Publication Data
Names: Korté, Steven, author. | Jeralds, Scott, illustrator.
Title: Drawing ghosts and ghouls with Scooby-Doo! / by Steve Korté ; illustrated by Scott Jeralds.
Description: North Mankato, Minnesota : Capstone Press, [2022] | Series: Drawing fun with Scooby-Doo! | Includes bibliographical references. | Audience: Ages 8–11 | Audience: Grades 4–6 | Summary: "Solve the mystery behind drawing Scooby-Doo's most popular ghosts and ghouls! With step-by-step instructions, you'll sketch the 10,000 Volt Ghost, the Creeper, the Ghost of Captain Cutler, and so much more! Best of all, drawing these classic Scooby characters has never been more fun and easy!"—Provided by publisher.
Identifiers: LCCN 2021030537 | ISBN 9781663958860 (hardcover)
Subjects: LCSH: Ghosts in art—Juvenile literature. | Monsters in art—Juvenile literature. | Ghosts in art—Juvenile literature. | Cartoon characters in art—Juvenile literature. | Drawing—Technique—Juvenile literature. |
Scooby-Doo (Fictitious character)—Juvenile literature.
Classification: LCC NC1764.8.M65 K673 2022 | DDC 743/.87—dc23
LC record available at https://lccn.loc.gov/2021030537

Editorial Credits
Christopher Harbo, Editor; Tracy Davies, Designer;
Katy LaVigne, Pre-Media Specialist

Design Elements
Shutterstock: BNP Design Studio, Ori Artiste, sidmay

Printed and bound in the USA. 4608

TABLE OF CONTENTS

Let's Draw Ghosts and Ghouls
with Scooby-Doo! 4

What You'll Need 5

The Green Ghosts 6

10,000 Volt Ghost 8

Phantom 10

Mummy of Anka 12

Black Knight 14

Ghost Clown 16

Redbeard's Ghost 18

The Creeper 20

Miner Forty Niner 22

Ghost of Captain Cutler 24

Ghost of Mr. Hyde 26

Escaping the Ghost Clown 28

More Drawing Fun! 32

More Scooby-Doo Fun! 32

LET'S DRAW GHOSTS AND GHOULS WITH SCOOBY-DOO!

It is a cold and rainy night in Crystal Cove. The five members of Mystery Inc. are staring at a dark and deserted Victorian mansion at the edge of town. They are huddled together, shivering from the cold. Three members of the gang—Fred Jones, Daphne Blake, and Velma Dinkley—take a few nervous steps toward the scary-looking house. Shaggy Rogers and his canine companion, Scooby-Doo, do not move from where they are standing. They both have worried looks on their faces.

Shaggy turns to Scooby-Doo. "We're out of here! Right, Scoob?" he says.

"Ruh-huh!" agrees Scooby-Doo.

Fred turns around. "Let's get in there, gang!" he says. "There have been reports of ghostly sounds coming from inside this deserted mansion."

"Like, I was afraid you were going to say that," says Shaggy with a sigh. "How about if Scoob and I stand guard outside the house? No sense in all five of us making this ghost angry."

Fred smiles at Shaggy and Scooby-Doo.

"Come on, guys," says Fred. "This is a job for the whole gang. It looks like we have a mystery to solve!"

Over the years, Mystery Inc. has battled a whole host of spooky creatures. Let's see what kind of ghosts and ghouls you can draw!

WHAT YOU'LL NEED

You are about to draw an especially ghastly group of ghosts and ghouls! But you'll need some basic tools to draw these frightening fiends. Gather the following supplies before starting your spooky art.

paper

You can get special drawing paper from art supply and hobby stores. But any type of blank, unlined paper will work fine.

pencils

Drawings should always be done in pencil first. Even the pros use them. If you make a mistake, it'll be easy to erase and redo it. Keep plenty of these essential drawing tools on hand.

pencil sharpener

To make clean lines, you need to keep your pencils sharp. Get a good pencil sharpener. You'll use it a lot.

erasers

As you draw, you're sure to make mistakes. Erasers give artists the power to turn back time and undo those mistakes. Get some high-quality rubber or kneaded erasers. They'll last a lot longer than pencil erasers.

black marker pens

When your drawing is ready, trace over the final lines with a black marker pen. The black lines will help make your characters stand out on the page.

colored pens and markers

Ready to finish your masterpiece? Bring your characters to life and give them some color with colored pencils or markers.

The Green Ghosts

Scooby-Doo is going to inherit a large fortune, but there's a catch. In order to collect the money, he and the rest of the Mystery Inc. gang must spend one night in a sinister mansion. Can the team survive a frightful night in a house that is haunted by two green ghosts?

1

drawing idea

Choose your two favorite members of Mystery Inc. and add them to your drawing of one of the Green Ghosts.

10,000 Volt Ghost

"Jinkies!" yells a frightened Velma when she encounters an electrified orange ghost that has yellow sparks shooting out of its body. It's the 10,000 Volt Ghost, and it has the power to melt metal objects. Some say that an electrician crossed the wrong wires at the Winterhaven Power Plant and became this sparking spookster.

1

dRawing idea
When you color the 10,000 Volt Ghost, add lots of bright yellow sparks around the edges of its body.

2

3

4

5

Phantom

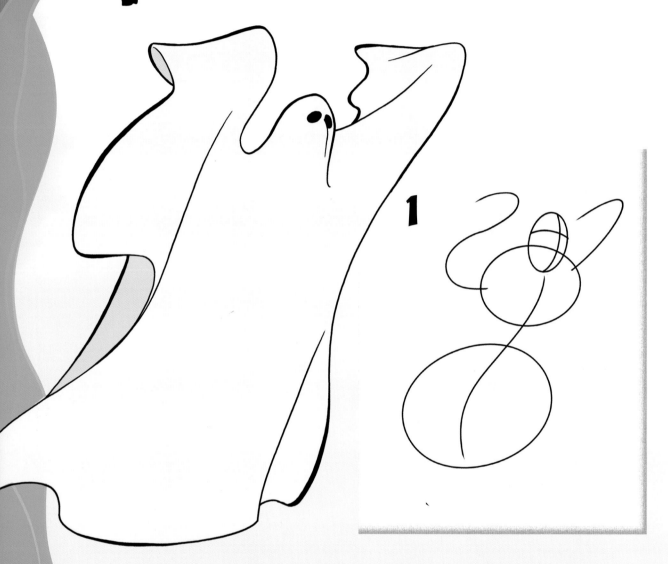

1

After the Mystery Inc. gang runs their boat aground on an island, they hike up to the creepy-looking Vasquez Castle to see if anyone can help them. It turns out that the castle is haunted by the Phantom. It's a creature covered in a long, flowing white robe, and it can walk through walls! But it's not all bad. Scooby and Shaggy are delighted to discover floating snacks inside the castle too!

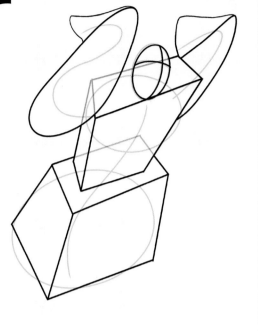

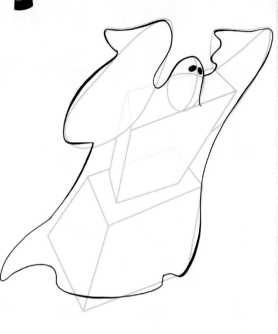

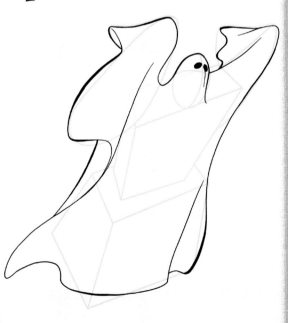

Mummy of Anka 1

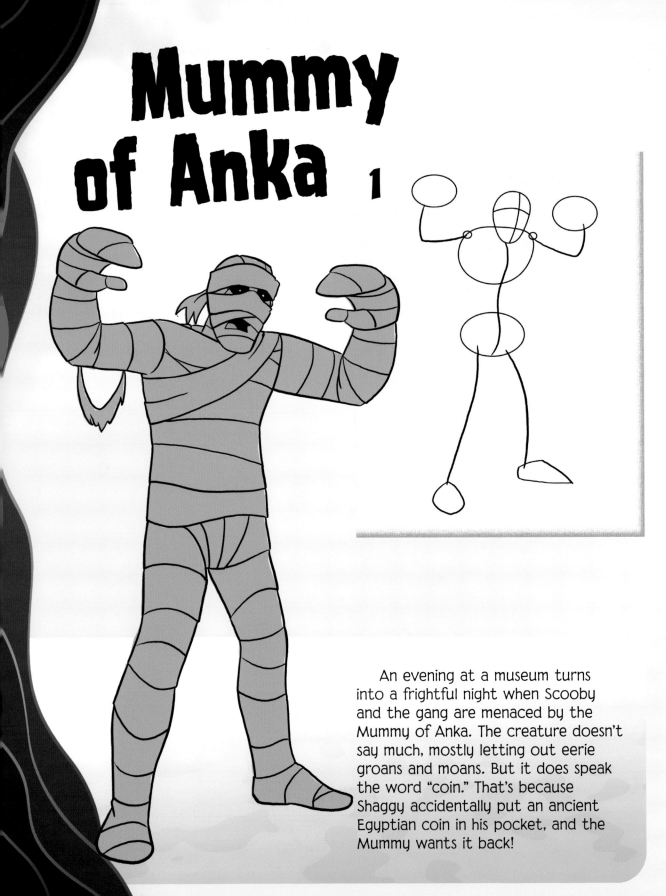

An evening at a museum turns into a frightful night when Scooby and the gang are menaced by the Mummy of Anka. The creature doesn't say much, mostly letting out eerie groans and moans. But it does speak the word "coin." That's because Shaggy accidentally put an ancient Egyptian coin in his pocket, and the Mummy wants it back!

2

3

4

5

Black Knight

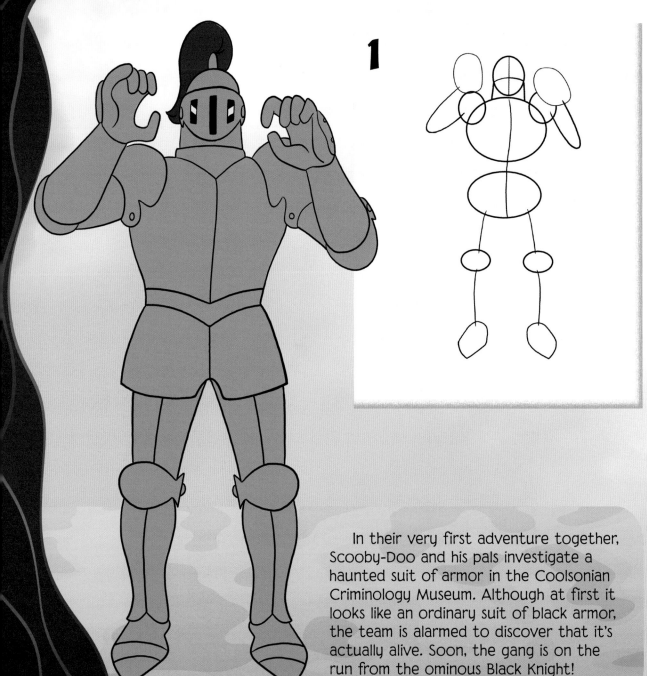

1

In their very first adventure together, Scooby-Doo and his pals investigate a haunted suit of armor in the Coolsonian Criminology Museum. Although at first it looks like an ordinary suit of black armor, the team is alarmed to discover that it's actually alive. Soon, the gang is on the run from the ominous Black Knight!

2

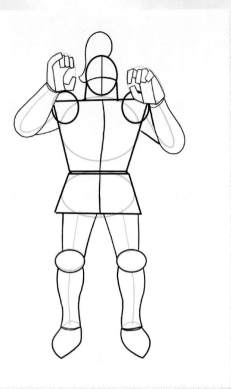

3

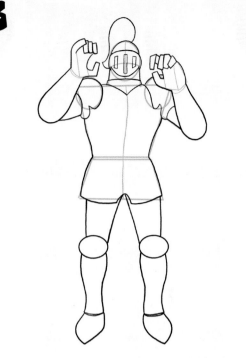

4

5

Ghost Clown

The Ghost Clown is haunting Barnstorm's Circus! Despite his silly-looking costume, this cackling clown is no joke. The Ghost Clown has an evil grin on his face, a menacing laugh, and glowing yellow eyes. He is also an expert hypnotist and uses a gold coin to hypnotize both Shaggy and Daphne! Will the hypnosis cure Shaggy of his endless appetite?

1

dRawing idea

The next time you draw the Ghost Clown, show him holding a gold coin in his hand as he hypnotizes Shaggy.

2

3

4

5

Redbeard's Ghost

1

"Ahhhhhhr!" cries out the ghost of Redbeard. With his pirate hat, his flowing, red beard, and his razor-sharp sword, this sinister swashbuckler cuts a mean figure. But when he starts robbing freighter ships near Skull Island, Scooby and the gang know they must set sail to solve a mystery.

2

3

4

5

The Creeper

"Let's go, gang! We have a mystery to solve!" Fred calls out when trouble rears its head in town. It's the hulking hunchbacked creature known as the Creeper. This giant, green-faced brute has a violent temper. And after the monster robs a bank and disrupts a school dance, it's up to Mystery Inc. to trap this ghastly ghoul.

1

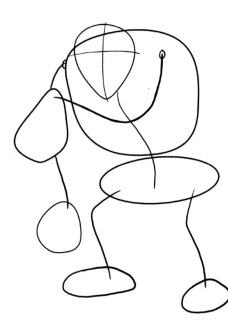

drawing idea
Show Fred standing bravely in front of the giant Creeper.

2

3

4

5

Miner Forty Niner

1

When Scooby and the gang journey to a deserted mining town called Gold City, they meet up with a 150-year-old ghost miner. His name is the Miner Forty Niner, and he has scared off all of Gold City's residents and tourists. Will he scare off Mystery Inc., too, when they go digging for clues in his mine?

2

3

4

5

Ghost of Captain Cutler

1

Rocky Point Beach is the perfect spot for a beach party. But while gobbling down some tasty snacks—including chocolate-covered hot dogs for Scooby and Shaggy—the gang's fun comes to an end. A glowing, green scuba suit suddenly crashes the party! Local residents say that this spook is the ghost of the long-dead sailor, Captain Cutler.

Ghost of Mr. Hyde

1

"Jeepers!" yells Daphne when she discovers the Ghost of Mr. Hyde inside the Mystery Machine. This unwelcome intruder has pasty, green skin, long, bony fingers, and an evil, cackling laugh. Even more creepy, this ghastly ghost can also climb up the walls of buildings to escape the Mystery Inc. gang!

2

3

4

5

Escaping the Ghost Clown

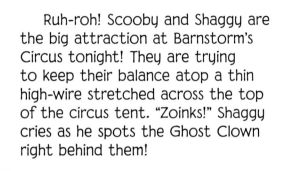

Ruh-roh! Scooby and Shaggy are the big attraction at Barnstorm's Circus tonight! They are trying to keep their balance atop a thin high-wire stretched across the top of the circus tent. "Zoinks!" Shaggy cries as he spots the Ghost Clown right behind them!

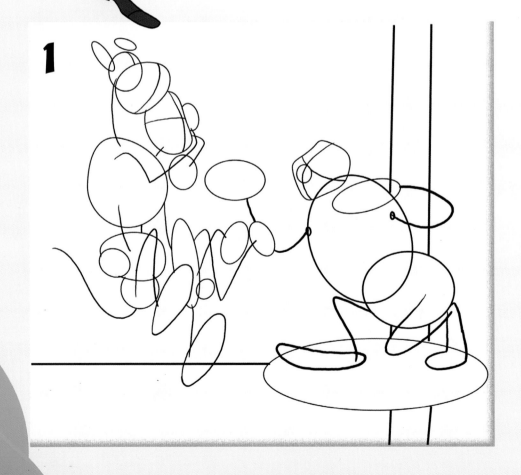

1

2

3

MORE DRAWING FUN!

Bird, Benjamin. *Food Doodles with Scooby-Doo!* North Mankato, MN: Capstone Press, 2017.

Harbo, Christopher. *10-Minute Drawing Projects.* North Mankato, MN: Capstone Press, 2020.

Sautter, Aaron. *How to Draw Batman and His Friends and Foes.* North Mankato, MN: Capstone Press, 2015.

MORE SCOOBY-DOO FUN!

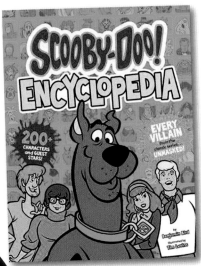

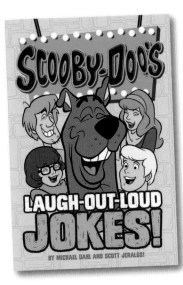